BRAIN TRAINING

for Reversals

b-d-p-q

Bridgette Sharp

ISBN-13: 978-1546367611

ISBN-10: 1546367616

What is Brain Training?

Brain Training consists of many different exercises designed to improve brain processing speed, hemispheric integration between the right and left sides of the brain, as well as internal brain timing and sequencing.

While the right brain identifies the color, the left brain is utilized to read the shapes, numbers and letters. As each exercise is done, the right and left brain must communicate to complete the task. This encourages new neurons to connect. Neurons that fire together wire together. Therefore, the more the exercises are done the stronger the neural connections, the quicker the brain responds.

Brain training is a natural way to make difficult mental tasks easier. Cognitive difficulties can often be a result of slow or lacking left and right brain communication. Using brain training exercises engages both hemispheres to communicate and work simultaneously. It also benefits the brain by improving memory, sequencing and processing speed.

The results are often remarkable. New information is easier to learn, remember and recall.

These mental exercises are wonderful for students young and old. Poor readers can greatly benefit from brain training. Professionals and those wishing to improve their memory and brain processing speed benefit greatly. Mental exercises are recommended for the aging to keep their brain young and to discourage dementia or other cognitive problems from developing.

Brain training exercises are used to help remediate cognitive problems related to Dyslexia, Dysgraphia, ADD, ADHD, Reading difficulties, Executive Functioning Skills, Dementia, Alzheimer's, Autism, Aspergers, Central Auditory Processing Disorder and Visual Processing Disorders.

Reversals

Although some letter and number reversals are considered normal for very young children just beginning to read, it's problematic and should be corrected as soon as it's noticed.

Using the techniques in this book, your student can improve visual processing skills, sequencing skills, improve visual tracking and lessen the occurrence of reversals.

It's important that your student 'read' the material found in the hemispheric integration girds and visual tracking lines correctly. Always do the activity beginning at the top, left corner, proceed right along the line then drop down to the starting character on the next line at the far left and 'read' across the line to the right again, just like reading a book line by line. In this way we are teaching and reinforcing visual tracking skills and visual discrimination.

This is a form of cognitive therapy, brain training, and can be used by therapists, teachers, tutors and parents to teach and reinforce important skills necessary for successful reading and writing.

Brain Training grids start at the top left corner and move right across the row. We then move to the row below the one completed and move left to right, continue in this fashion, ending with the bottom right square of the grid. In this example the squares are numbered for you.

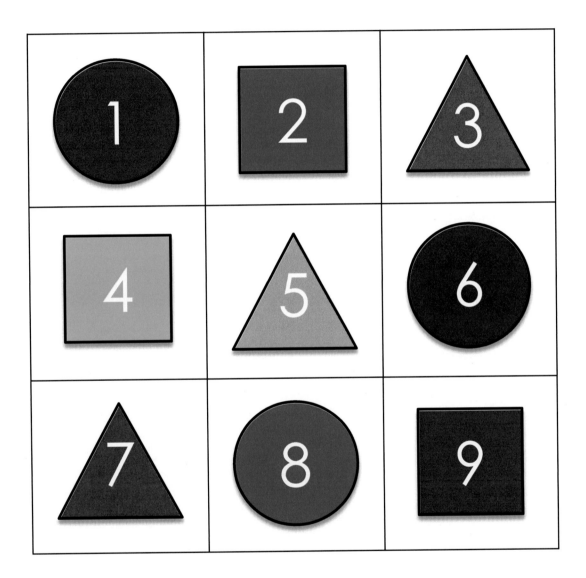

The grids in this book are arranged systematically from simple to more complex, therefore they should be completed in order. Each grid should be done multiple times to assure mastery before moving to the next grid.

Name the Color. Start at the top left square of the grid and name the colors. Record your time and try to beat it!

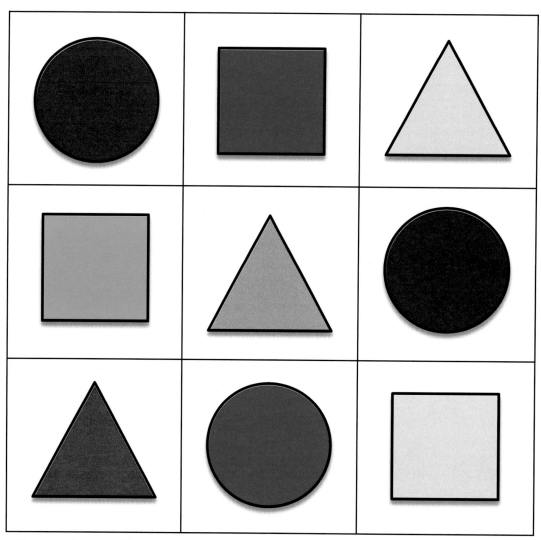

Record your times here!

_____   _____   _____

_____   _____   _____

_____   _____   _____

Name the Number. Start at the top left square of the grid and name the numbers. Record your time and try to beat it!

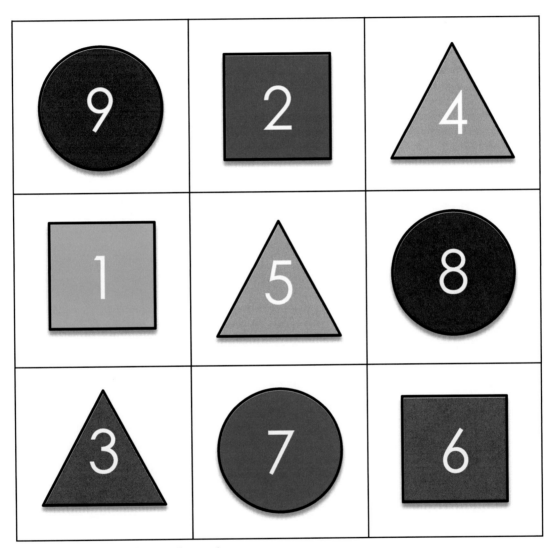

Record your times here!

_____   _____   _____

_____   _____   _____

_____   _____   _____

Name the Color and Number. Start at the top left square of the grid and name the color first and then the number. i.e. "Red Eight" Record your time and try to beat it!

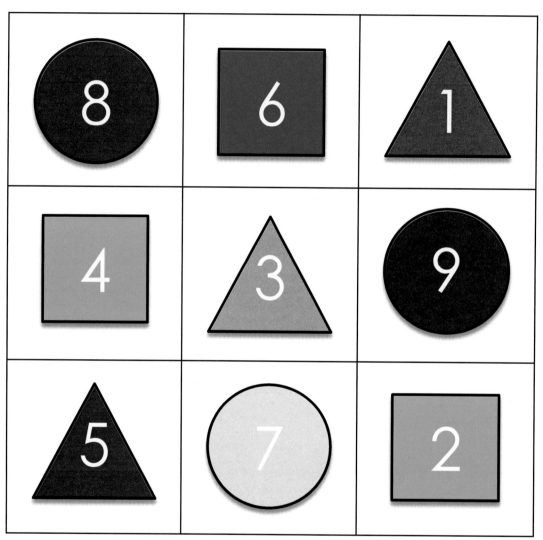

Record your times here!

_____   _____   _____

_____   _____   _____

_____   _____   _____

Name the Color, Shape and Number. Start at the top left square of the grid and name the color first and then the shape followed by the number in the shape. i.e. "Red Circle Eight" Record your time and try to beat it!

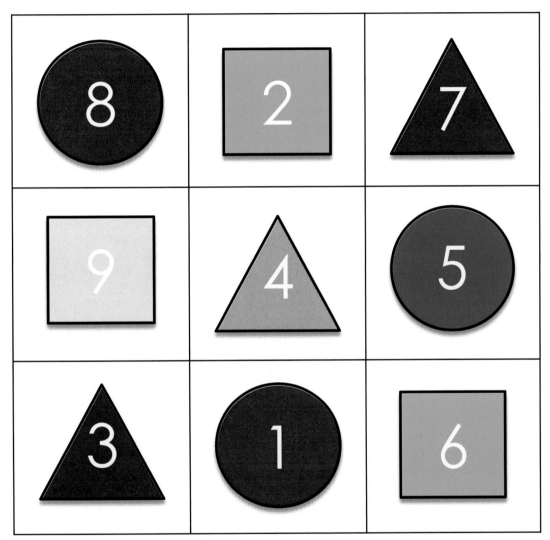

Record your times here!

_____   _____   _____

_____   _____   _____

_____   _____   _____

Start here!

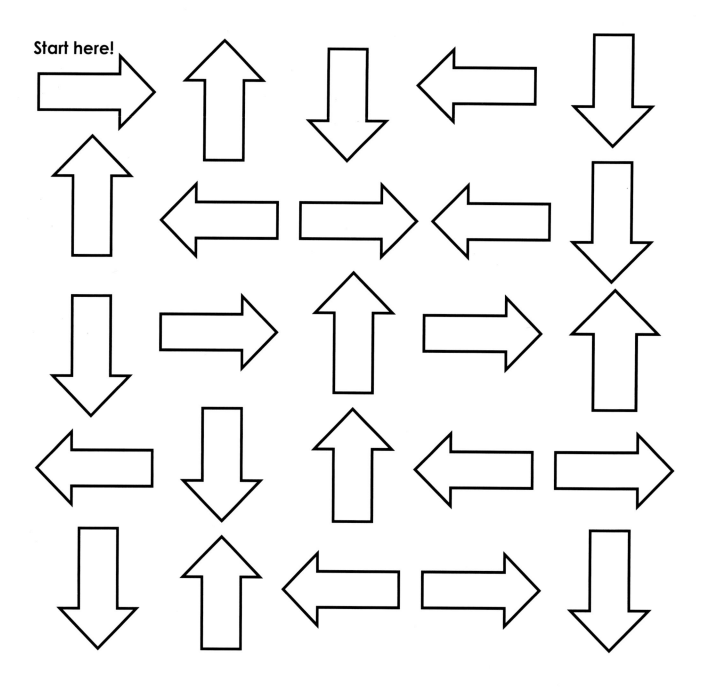

Cognitive Arrows

1. Starting at the top left corner, name the direction each arrow is facing. i.e. "right, up, down, left, down..." Record times here:

_____ _____ _____ _____ _____

_____ _____ _____ _____ _____

Start here!

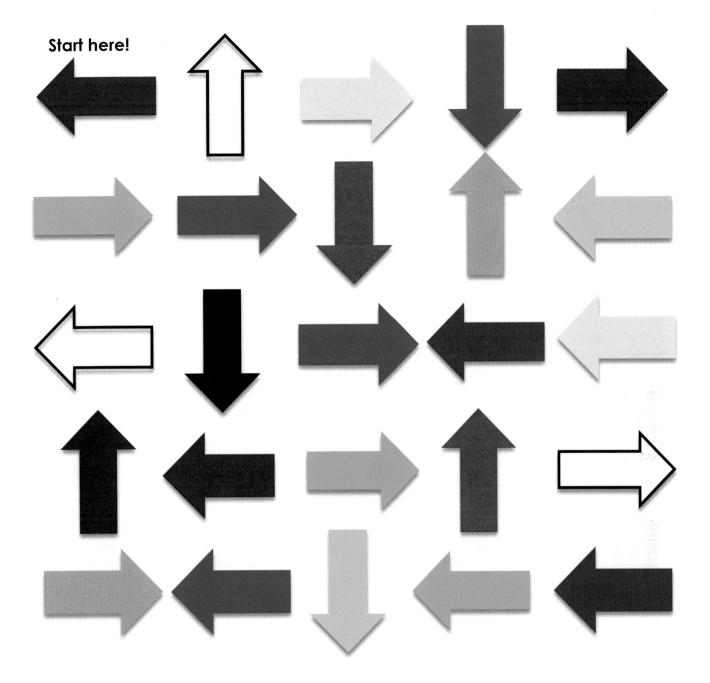

Color Cognitive Arrows

1. Starting at the top left corner, name the color of the arrow and then the direction each arrow is facing. i.e. "red left, white up…" Record times here:

    _____ _____ _____ _____ _____ _____

2. Now name the direction first and then the color. i.e. " left red, up white…"

    _____ _____ _____ _____ _____ _____

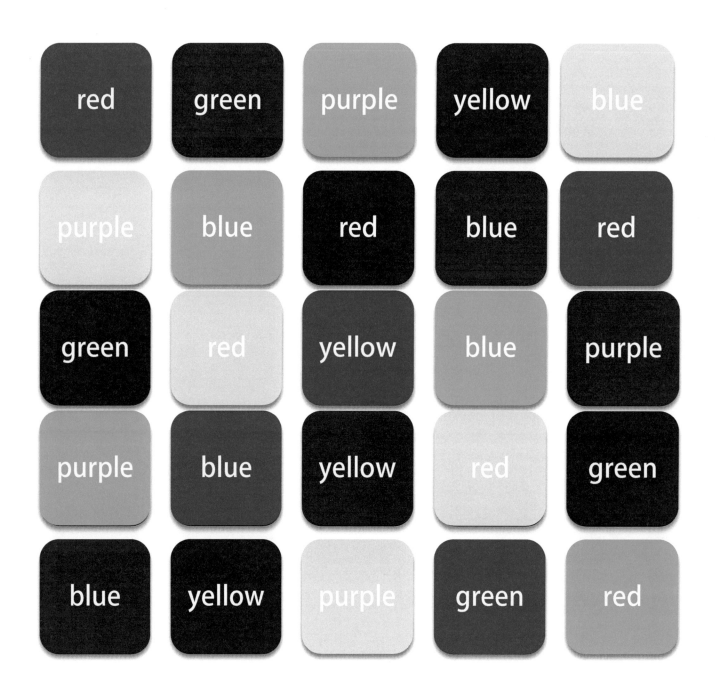

Cognitive Colors

1. Name the color of the square and then read the color word in the square. i.e. "blue red, red green..." Record times here:

    _____   _____   _____   _____   _____   _____

2. Now read the color word first and then the color of the square. i.e. red blue, green red..."

    _____   _____   _____   _____   _____   _____

Start here!

Cognitive Shapes

1. Starting at the top left corner, name the large shape and color and then the small shape and color. i. e. "red square green square, yellow star white heart, blue circle red circle…" Record times here:

   _____   _____   _____   _____   _____

2. Now repeat the exercise in the reverse order; name the small shape and color first and then the large shape and color. i.e. : green square red square, white heart yellow star, red circle blue circle…"

   _____   _____   _____   _____   _____

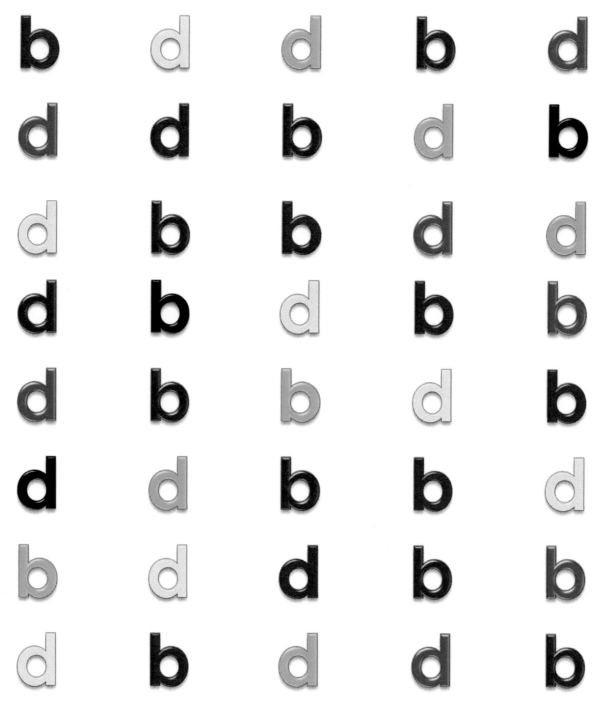

bd Colors

1. Starting at the top left corner, name each color and letter.

2. Now name the letter first and then the color.

3. Use a stopwatch and time yourself. Try to get faster and faster each time you do it!

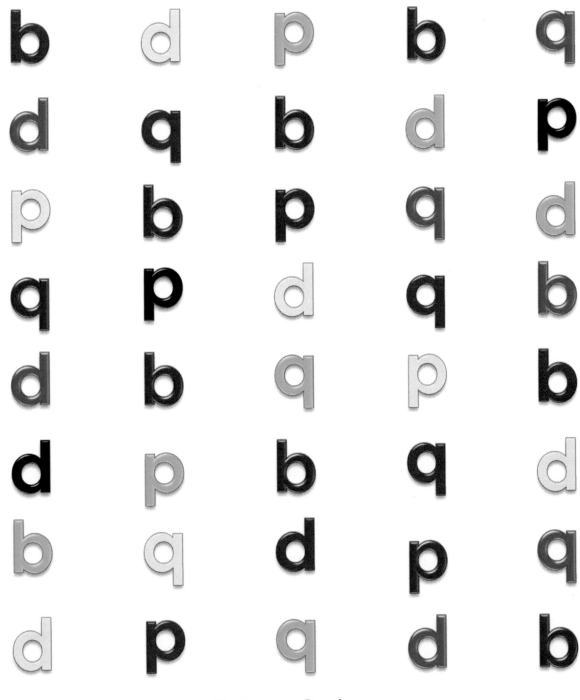

Bdpq Colors

1. Starting at the top left corner, name each color and letter. i.e. " red B, yellow D, green P, purple B..."

2. Now name the letter first and then the color. i.e. " B red, D yellow, P green..."

3. Use a stopwatch and time yourself. Try to get faster and faster each time you do it!

bp qd pp bd pq

db bq bb bd pb

pd db pd dq dd

pq pp dp pq pb

qd bq qq pq bq

bd pb bd pq dd

db pq pd pq bq

bd qp pq db bb

Bdpq Colors 2

1. Starting at the top left corner, name each letter in order. i.e. "bpqdpp..."

2. Now name the color and the letters. i.e. "blue B, red P, yellow Q..."

3. Use a stopwatch and time yourself. Try to get faster and faster each time you do it!

Bd96 Colors

1. Starting at the top left corner, name each number and letter. i.e. " Blue 6, red D, pink 9, yellow q, green 6, green D..."

2. Now name the letter first and then the number. i.e. " Red D, blue 6, yellow q, pink 9..."

3. Use a stopwatch and time yourself. Try to get faster and faster each time you do it!

b ↓ ↑ **d** **p** ← **b** → **q** ↓

↑ **d** ← **q** **b** ↓ → **d** **p** →

p ← **b** → **p** ↑ **q** ← **d** ↓

q ↓ ↑ **p** ← **d** → **q** ↑ **b**

← **d** **b** ↓ **q** → **p** ← ↑ **b**

→ **d** **p** ← **b** ↑ ↓ **q** **d** ←

b ↑ **q** ↓ ← **d** ← **p** **q** →

← **d** ↑ **p** → **q** **d** ← ↓ **b**

Bdqp Arrows

1. Starting at the top left corner, name each letter and the arrow direction. i.e. "b down, d up, p left, b right…"

2. Now name the letter first, then the arrow direction and lastly the color of the letter. i.e. " b down red, d up yellow, p left green…"

3. Use a stopwatch and time yourself. Try to get faster and faster each time you do it!

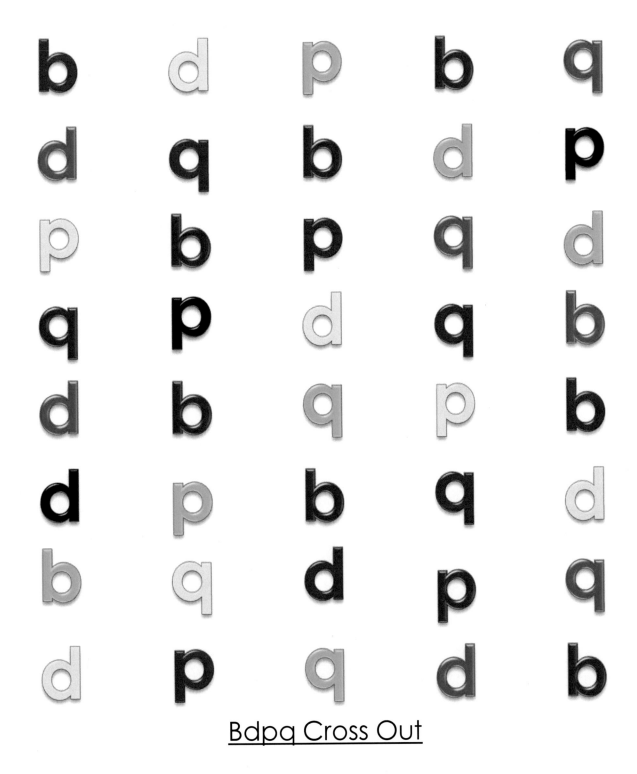

Bdpq Cross Out

1. Slide a page protector over the page and use a write on, wipe off marker.

2. Starting at the top left corner, move from left to right, like reading a book;

    a. Cross out the letter b.
    b. Circle the letter d.
    c. Draw a slash through the letter p.
    d. Underline letter q.

Bdpq Cross Out 2

1. Slide a page protector over the page and use a write on, wipe off marker.

2. Starting at the top left corner, move from left to right, like reading a book;

    a. Cross out when d comes first.
    b. Circle when 6 comes first.
    c. Underline when b comes first.
    d. Slash through when 9 comes first.

bp   qd   pp   bd   pq

db   bq   bb   bd   pb

pd   db   pd   dq   dd

pq   pp   dp   pq   pb

qd   bq   qq   pq   bq

bd   pb   bd   pq   dd

db   pq   pd   pq   bq

bd   qp   pq   db   bb

Bdpq Cross Out 3

1.   Slide a page protector over the page and use a write on, wipe off marker.
2.   Starting at the top left corner, move from left to right, like reading a book;

    a.   Cross out when the letter b comes first.
    b.   Circle when the letter d comes first.
    c.   Underline when p comes first.
    d.   Slash through when q comes first.

belly button b

Beginning at the left of each line, see how quickly you can 'read' the line from left to right and put a dot (belly button) in the center of each **b**. There are six in each line.

Place a page protector over the page and use a write on, wipe off marker for repeated use.

bpqddpbqbdpdbqbpbpq

qdpbpdbqpbbpdqbqpbd

pbpdqbdbpqdbddbqpbp

dbpqdbdbpdbqdpbqbpd

bdpqbdpqbdpqbpdqbbd

ddpbqbdpbpqddbdbpqb

pbdbpqbdbdqpddpqbpb

bdbpqpdqbpdbdpqdpbb

Visual Tracking d

Beginning at the left of each line, see how quickly you can 'read' the line from left to right and circle each **d**. There are six in each line.

Place a page protector over the page and use a write on, wipe off marker for repeated use.

dpqddpbqbdpdbqbpbpd

qdpbpdbqdbbpdqbdpbd

pbpdqbdbpqdbddbqdbp

dbpqdbdbpdbqdpbqbpd

bdpdbdpqbdpqbpdqbbd

ddpbqbdpbpqddbdbpqb

pbdbpqbdbdqpddpqdpb

bdbpqpdqbpdbdpqdpdb

Visual Tracking p

Beginning at the left of each line, see how quickly you can 'read' the line from left to right and slash through each **p**. There are six in each line.

Place a page protector over the page and use a write on, wipe off marker for repeated use.

dppddpbqbdpdbqbpbpd

pdpbpdbqdbbpdqpdpbd

pbpdqbpbpqdbpdbqdbp

dbpqdpdbpdbqdpbpbpd

bdpdbdpqbdpqbpdpbbp

ddpbqbdpbpqdpbdbpqp

pbdbpqbdpdqpddpqdpb

bdbpqpdqbpdbdpqdpdp

<u>Visual Tracking q</u>

Beginning at the left of each line, see how quickly you can 'read' the line from left to right and cross out each **q**. There are six in each line.

Place a page protector over the page and use a write on, wipe off marker for repeated use.

qppqdpbqbdpqbqbpbpq

pqpbpqbqqbbpdqpdpqd

qbpdqbpbpqdqpdbqdqp

dqpqdpdbpqbqdpqpbpq

bqpdqdpqbdpqqpdpbqp

qdpbqbdpqpqdpbqbpqp

pqdbpqbqpdqpddpqdpq

bqbpqpdqqpdbdpqdpqp

bdpq

Beginning at the left of each line, see how quickly you can 'read' the line from left to right and:

      1. Put a belly button in each b
      2. Circle each d
      3. Slash through each p
      4. Cross out each q

bpqddpqqbdpdbqbpbpq

qdpbpdbqpbqpdqbqpbd

pbpdqbdbpqdbdqbqpbp

dbpqdbdqpdbqdpbqbpd

bdpqbdpqbdpqbpdqbbd

ddpbqbdpbpqddbdbpqb

pbdbpqbdbdqpddpqbpb

bdbpqpdqbpdbdpqdpbb

Visual Tracking & Discrimination

Look at the first symbol (letter, number or symbol) and then "read" the line from left to right and circle all 5 of the matching symbols.

Place a page protector over the page and use a write on, wipe off marker for repeated use.

b   bdddddbdddbddddbddddbddddddd

d   bbbbbddbbbbdbbbbbbdbbbbbbbdbbbbbb

p   qqqqpqqpqqqqpqqqqqpqqqqqqpqqqqq

q   pppqpppqppppqppppqppppppqpppppppp

6   99996996999996999996996999999999

9   66666966666966666669666666966669

b   bdpqddpqbppqdqdbpdddqbpqdbpddqd

d   bdbbpbqbbdpqbdbbpqbdqbbpbbdqbbp

p   pqdqqbbqdqpqdpbqpqqqdbqqbdpqqqq

Visual Tracking & Discrimination

Look at the first word and then "read" the line from left to right and circle all 5 occurrences of the matching word.

Place a page protector over the page and use a write on, wipe off marker for repeated use.

bed   bbededebedbbdebedbdebeddebededb

dad   bdadapadadbaddadbapadadbedadapad

pod   podobogpodqodpodbogpoddopodqodp

quad   aquaduabqquadpaquadaquadquabquad

69   66999669966666699999669999966669

96   66699966666999996999966666696696

deb   bbeddebbededbedebdbdebbedebdebd

bad   dadabadbbdbadadabadaddbadbbadadd

pup   qpuqpuppuuqpuppupquqpupuqupupqu

Visual Tracking & Discrimination

Look at the sentences and circle every **b**. You don't have to read the sentences, just move from left to right.

Place a page protector over the page and use a write on, wipe off marker for repeated use.

My big, bad brown dog ate all the bread.

The bed spread is black, blue and brown.

Blowing bubbles in the back yard is fun.

Aunt Tabby has a baby kitten in the bathtub.

The baby is climbing out of her crib.

When it was bedtime I put my book back in my book bag. I ate a bologna and banana sandwich with blue bug juice. My baby brother had bug juice on his bib. He blew blue bubbles out of his nose. Aunt Tabby put my blue brother into the bathtub.

Visual Tracking & Discrimination

Look at the sentences and underline every **d**. You don't have to read the sentences, just move from left to right.

Place a page protector over the page and use a write on, wipe off marker for repeated use.

My big, bad brown dog ate all the bread.

The red bed spread is hidden in the sand.

Dad laid the ladder by the dark door.

The dirty duck dove into the pond.

"Daddy long legs are not spiders," said dad.

My pet duck is named Daisy. Daisy does tricks. She likes to ride in my red wagon. Daisy dances to loud music and waddles when she walks. Ducks do not get sad. Daisy likes to eat dog food. She digs in the yard and even laid an egg.

Visual Tracking & Discrimination

Look at the sentences and slash through every **p**. You don't have to read the sentences, just move from left to right.

Place a page protector over the page and use a write on, wipe off marker for repeated use.

My pencil is next to the pizza behind the lamp.

The grasshopper is hopping on an apple.

Penny the pony pranced in the parade.

My pet poodle is napping in the teepee.

Polly spilled her soup and now it's dripping off the table.

I have a pet parrot who thinks he's a pirate. Pickle is his name. He eats pizza and plays the piano. Pickle climbs up a rope to the top of my toy ship. He makes sounds like a sheep, pig and pony. Pickle can walk like a penguin.

Visual Tracking & Discrimination

Look at the sentences and cross out every **q**. You don't have to read the sentences, just move from left to right.

Place a page protector over the page and use a write on, wipe off marker for repeated use.

The queen quit eating spaghetti squash.

She quickly quieted her squealing pig.

Don't squeeze the square marshmallows.

I have a question about the quilt.

I can quote the queen.

I need quarters to play the quarterback game.

Mom made a quilt with quilt squares.

I questioned her with a pop quiz.

She is quite quiet at night.

Visual Tracking & Discrimination

Look at the sentences and : 1. Circle every **b**
2. Underline every **d**
3. Slash through every **p**
4. Cross out every **q**

Place a page protector over the page and use a write on, wipe off marker for repeated use.

My big, bad brown dog ate all the bread.

The red bed spread is hidden in the sand.

The queen quit eating spaghetti squash.

The grasshopper is hopping on an apple.

Aunt Tabby has a baby kitten in the bathtub.

My pet duck is named Debby. Debby does tricks. She likes to ride in my big, red wagon. Debby dances to loud music and quacks when she waddles. Ducks do not get sad. Debby likes to eat pickles. She digs up bugs in the yard and even laid an egg.

Arrow Maze

Complete the maze by following the arrows.

Visual discrimination & visual tracking, Directionality, Following Directions

Place a page protector over the page and use a write on, wipe off marker for repeated use.

Enter

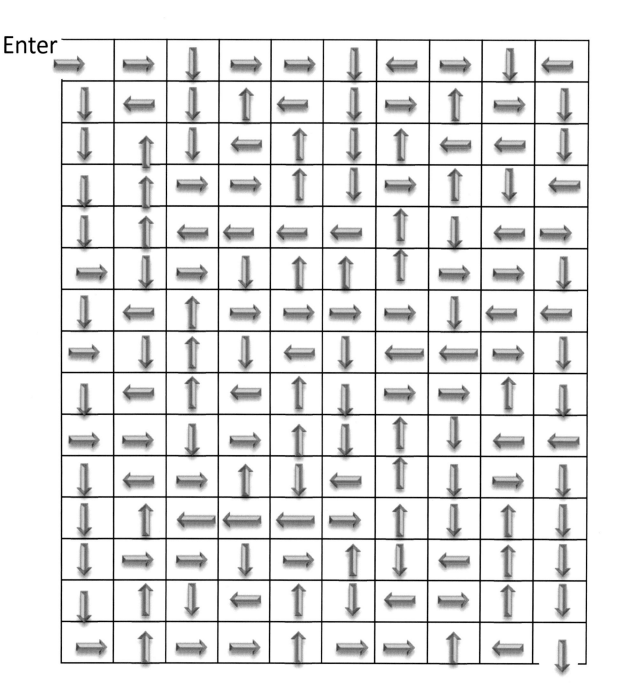

Exit

b Maze

Complete the maze by following the letter **b**.
Visual discrimination & visual tracking, Directionality, Following Directions

Place a page protector over the page and use a write on, wipe off marker for repeated use.

Enter

b	b	b	b	b	d	b	b	b	b
d	d	d	d	b	d	b	d	d	b
b	b	b	d	b	b	b	d	d	b
b	d	b	d	d	d	d	b	b	b
b	d	b	b	b	b	b	b	d	d
b	d	d	d	d	d	d	d	d	d
b	b	d	b	b	b	b	b	b	b
d	b	d	b	d	d	d	d	d	b
b	b	d	b	b	d	b	b	b	b
b	d	d	d	b	d	d	d	d	d
b	b	d	b	b	d	b	b	b	d
d	b	b	b	d	d	d	d	b	b

Exit

d Maze

Complete the maze by following the letter **d**.
Visual discrimination & visual tracking, Directionality, Following Directions

Place a page protector over the page and use a write on, wipe off marker for repeated use.

d	d	d	d	d	d	b	d	d	d
d	b	b	b	b	d	b	d	b	d
d	d	d	b	b	d	d	d	b	d
b	b	d	b	b	b	b	b	d	d
b	b	d	d	d	d	b	d	d	b

Enter d | b | b | b | b | d | b | d | b | d **Exit**

d	b	d	d	d	d	b	d	b	d
d	b	d	b	b	b	b	d	b	d
d	b	d	d	d	d	b	d	d	d
d	d	b	b	b	d	d	b	b	b
b	d	d	d	b	b	d	b	d	d
b	b	b	d	d	d	d	b	d	d

p Maze

Complete the maze by following the letter **p**.

Visual discrimination & visual tracking, Directionality, Following Directions

Place a page protector over the page and use a write on, wipe off marker for repeated use.

Enter   Exit

p	p	p	p	q	p	p	p	p	p
q	q	q	p	q	p	p	q	q	q
q	q	q	p	p	q	p	p	p	p
p	p	p	q	p	q	q	q	q	p
p	q	p	q	p	q	p	p	p	p
p	q	p	p	p	q	p	q	q	q
p	q	q	q	q	q	p	p	p	q
p	p	q	p	p	p	q	q	p	q
q	p	q	p	q	p	p	q	p	p
p	p	q	p	q	q	p	q	q	p
p	q	q	p	q	q	p	q	p	p
p	p	p	p	q	q	p	p	p	q

q Maze

Complete the maze by following the letter **q**.
Visual discrimination & visual tracking, Directionality, Following Directions

Place a page protector over the page and use a write on, wipe off marker for repeated use.

q	q	q	p	p	q	q	q	q	q
q	p	q	q	q	p	p	p	p	q
q	p	p	p	p	q	q	q	p	q
q	q	p	q	q	q	p	q	q	q
p	q	p	q	p	p	p	p	p	p

Enter

q	q	p	q	p	q	q	q	q	q	Exit

p	p	q	q	p	q	p	p	p	p
q	q	q	p	p	q	q	p	p	p
q	p	p	p	p	p	p	q	q	p
q	q	p	q	q	p	p	p	p	q
p	p	p	p	q	q	p	q	q	q
p	q	q	q	p	q	q	q	p	p

Word Reading

Read each word. Keep practicing until you can read them all easily.

bib	pub	sob	quiz
did	grub	sod	dog
bad	bubble	aqua	big
dad	dud	pup	spot
pad	quib	pop	squid
quad	quid	pip	drip
squid	pod	dip	cup
bop	dob	did	pug
pap	quit	bib	pig
Bob	sip	pig	brag
dab	sap	queen	plod

OTHER BOOKS BY BRIDGETTE SHARP

Brain Training COLORS- Kindle

Brain Training SHAPES –Kindle

Brain Training NUMBERS—Kindle

Brain Training PHONICS - Kindle

12 Weeks to Superior Memory – Kindle

Neuromotor Brain Training Exercises – Kindle

Cognitive Training Exercises – Kindle Kindle

Brain Balancing Hemispheric Integration - Kindle

Brain Training ABC's & 123's: Kindergarten Readiness – Kindle

Brain Training Capital Letters – Kindle Kindle

Brain Training Sight Words: 100 HF Words –

Brain Training Letter Sounds – Kindle

Brain Training CVC Words – Kindle

Brain Training Lower Case Letters - Kindle

Hacking Consciousness: Life's Little Cheat Codes - Kindle

Brain Training Exercises to Boost Brain Power: for Improved Memory, Focus & Cognitive Function- Kindle

12 Weeks to Superior Memory & Mental Clarity: The Ultimate Cognitive Enhancement Program

Brain Training ABC's & 123's: Kindergarten Readiness Workbook

Brain Training Boot Camp: Be Sharper, Faster, Smarter

Brain Training Exercises to Boost Brain Power: for Improved Memory, Focus & Cognitive Function

Brain Training First Grade Sight Words: First Grade High Frequency Words

Brain Training Phonics: A Whole Brain Approach to Learning Phonics

Brain Training Second Grade Sight Words

Brain Training Sight Words: 1000 High Frequency Words Every Student Must Know

Brain Training Sight Words Grades 1 -3

Brain Training Sight Words Grades 4 - 6

OTHER BOOKS BY BRIDGETTE SHARP

Brain Training Sight Words Upper Levels

Brain Training Third Grade Sight Words

Creative Exercises for Boosting Brain Power: Creatively Boost Memory, Focus, Attention and Brain Balancing

Hacking Consciousness: Life's Little Cheat Codes

Hands On Phonemic Awareness Workbook

Hands On Reading Drills Workbook

Raise Reading Scores in 5 Minutes a Day

Reading Drills Kids Need to be Fast Readers: Raise Reading Test Scores

Sight Word Phonics: Learn Phonics with High Frequency Words

Sight Word Spinners 1000: Simple & Fun Practice for 1000 High Frequency Words

Sight Word Spinners Grades 1 – 3: Simple & Fun Practice for 300 High Frequency Words

Soul Lessons Adult Coloring Book

Spirit Animals Adult Coloring Book

ONE LAST THING

If you enjoyed this book or found it useful I'd be very grateful if you'd post a short review on Amazon. Your support really does make a difference. I read all of the reviews personally and use the information to produce future publications.

68173322R00025

Made in the USA
Lexington, KY
03 October 2017